GO LASSIE GO

A Story of Life

Christine
Brennan Mulvaney

To: Mary Ellen,
Enjoy!
Christine Mulvaney

D1367922

More copies available at www.Amazon.com

ISBN 13: 978-1523791378
ISBN: 1523791373

First Edition: April 2016

10 9 8 7 6 5 4 3 2 1

Table of Contents

Go Lassie Go

"Oh the summertime is coming and the leaves are softly blooming on the wild mountainside all around the blooming heather — will you go lassie go — and we'll all go together."

Cover photo is the first day Christine Mulvaney arrived in America. She was standing on her aunt's front porch.

Acknowledgments

I want to thank Mary Reilly for all the guidance she has given me. When we met for lunch in Florida I showed her what I had written (which was only 10–15 pages long). She told me to keep on going, to not stop writing. She also put me in touch with Mike Farragher, who had written several books.

I would also like to thank Mike. We met a few times during a "Books in the Basement" writing group, and over several months he gave me a lot of advice. Then I was introduced to Laura Ginsberg, an editor. She took my writing and went over everything, and we met several times. She helped me to stay focused on my story, and she told me to not give up and to always keep trying. I couldn't have done this without her.

Then there's Noel, Lily, Maggie, Ellen, and the rest of my family for being so helpful in jogging my memory on certain events and people. They helped me put people and places together.

I couldn't have done this without the help of all of these wonderful people. I thank them all very much.

Cast of Characters

All my life I have always thought about my early childhood. I look back and think about where I came from and how I have gotten to where I am today. I still get flashbacks. My mind is filled with so many memories of my family and how they persevered during such hard and sad times. I was born in a small town called Derry Cough in County Roscommon, Ireland. My parents were Mary Ellen Cregg and John Brennan. There were nine children in our family — seven girls and two boys. Starting with the oldest: Elizabeth (Lily), Patrick (Pakie), Mary Ellen (Nellie), Gertrude (Terry), (Winnie/Una) Attracta, Bernard (Noel), Margaret (Maggie) and Christina (Christine). I started putting the "e" on the end of my name when I came to America and started going to school. I thought it was shorter to say and sounded softer.

About my Mother

There are many things I can remember vividly about my childhood, and then there are some things that were told to me by my family. One of the hardest was that my mother died when I was only 2 years old. They told me she went to the hospital in Boyle and was there for over a year. I never saw her again. I didn't understand what was happening because I was too young. My father used to visit her regularly. He travelled 7 miles to the hospital in a horse and buggy to see her. Then, after visiting her, he would go to town and the local shops to buy groceries, flour, sugar, and tea and bring it all back home to us. Lily, who was 14 at the time, and Pakie, who was 12, would take turns riding the only bike we had to go back and forth to the hospital to see her. Lily said my mother was kept in a separate ward from the rest of the hospital. The hospital would keep all the patients with consumption together in the same ward and would keep the windows open for her and the other patients to get fresh air. Sometimes she would send used clothes home with my father for us. She died of consumption or what is now called TB. Her only concern was to keep us warm back on the farm. She never realized how contagious the disease was.

She was laid out in a coffin at the hospital because they didn't want the consumption to spread. Lily said the room was very small, and she, my father, and Pakie were the only people there. Lily told me she went up to the casket and that my mother looked so beautiful. Lily said my mother's skin was so white and smooth against her black hair. Lily was so shocked when she kissed her on the cheek because my mother was ice cold. Everything was so hard on them all. My mother was only 38 years old. They brought the casket back to the graveyard near our farm where everyone from that area gets buried. Lily said we were all there dressed in our Sunday best, and, after the ceremony, everyone had to throw dirt into the open grave. Everyone did this, but Pakie was so upset that he began shaking and crying and was so overwhelmed he tried to jump into the grave to be with her. My father and cousins grabbed him and held him tightly until the service was over. The priest was there and gave his blessing. My mother's gravesite is at the top of the hill along with my father and Uncle Jimmy.

The only picture we have of our mother.

This is my father, Noel, Winnie, and Terry standing in front of our farmhouse in Ireland.

Regarding the House

After my mother died, time went by, and my father did the best he could. My older sisters and brothers took over doing all the chores, such as getting water from the well, cleaning the house, getting turf for the fire, and doing the laundry. Lily told me the laundry was done in a big washtub outside, and then she would hang or drape the clothes over the bushes to dry.

We lived in a typical Irish cottage. We had three rooms. The kitchen was located in the middle with one bedroom on each side. One bedroom was my parents' and the other one was for the rest of us, plus my Uncle Jimmy (my father's brother who also lived with us). After my mother's passing Pakie moved his bed into my father's room, and that's where he slept. In our room we had two settle beds, as they were called, built into the wall, and the other two beds were lined up in the room. We slept with at least three to a bed, and when it got very cold we (the younger kids) would jump into bed with Uncle Jimmy just to keep warm. There was no bathroom, so we could use a pot or go outside — which, in the winter, we really hated. Our house was heated with turf in the fireplace, which we had to gather daily. We had a thatched roof and no running water. We would get our water from the well. In the kitchen the floor was made of concrete and there was a large table where we ate. There was also a large fireplace, which was kept heated all day. The cooking was done in the fireplace where we had a couple of large pots hung on hooks to boil water and cook the food. There was no gate for protection near the fireplace, and one day I was playing and I ran and fell into the fireplace and burned my hand. I still have a bad scar on my finger from that day. Taking care of the farm was hard work, and so was trying to take care of us younger ones. They tell me now that I was a real hell-raiser! Always tearing through the house and running in the fields. They said I would never comb the back of my hair because I used to say to them, "Who can see the back of my head?!"

There were many chickens and other animals around our house. Nellie, Winnie, and Terry would work tirelessly collecting the eggs and hiding them in the bales of hay until market day. They would collect all of the eggs and then walk or ride the bicycle into town to sell them. One day when they went to get the eggs the dogs had gotten into them and had eaten every egg. Boy, was everyone mad! You know the Irish temper! They chased the dogs all around the farm and even into the woods until they couldn't run any longer. Most of the dogs got away, but one or two of them were caught and taken immediately to the lake and drowned. Usually our dog Daisy would sleep in the kitchen near the heat — but she didn't sleep in the kitchen that night! Eventually she was let back in the house.

Every Saturday night was bath night. Noel and Pakie would bring in the big washtub and put it right on the kitchen floor where we would take turns taking our bath. My sisters always put the younger ones in first while the water was still nice and hot and clean. By the time it was the older ones' turn, they changed the water to make it clean again. The boys never wanted to get in the tub, but my father always made them. It was a ritual because you had to look nice and clean for church the next morning. Everyone had to go to church. No one could miss mass on Sunday.

Holiday Surprises

One Christmas I was about five or six years old, and we were all in the kitchen: my father, brothers, and sisters. We were all eating dinner, talking, and laughing. My Uncle Jimmy was there, and he was telling us stories of when he and my father were young and about all the trouble they used to get into. We would listen and laugh. Uncle Jimmy never married, and he always lived with us.

One of my sisters told me Santa came and left me my Christmas present in the bedroom. My eyes were wide open, and I couldn't talk. I was so excited I ran into the bedroom and started looking all around the room. I lifted all the covers on the beds, pulled up the sheets, and then I knew the only place left was under the beds, but I didn't want to look there because I knew there would be a lot of cat hair under there. But at that point I didn't care. I got down on my knees and started looking under each bed. I would stick my fingers in and take a quick look but found nothing. Then finally I went to the bed where I slept — I bent down looked in and saw something!! I didn't care anymore — I just stuck my head under and put my arm in and felt around, and I finally found something and grabbed it to pull it out. It was all covered with cat hair. I slid it out and wiped it off with my dress and then shook the rest of the cat hair off myself, that was when I looked down at the box, and I couldn't believe that Santa didn't forget me. I could hardly breathe, and I started running for the kitchen. Just as I got there I tripped on the doorway and fell. The box went flying and so did I. As it hit the floor the top went flying off and the box opened up. Inside the box was a pair of old men's shoes. Suddenly, everything went quiet — I looked at my father and older siblings, and they were in shock at what happened. Well...one of my sisters thought it would be funny. She never meant for it to hurt me. But I was crying and devastated. They all felt bad. My father sat me on his lap and gave me a real

Christmas present. It was beautiful orange tissue paper with a REAL orange inside of it — that was the tradition at the time. I gently tore the tissue away and slowly ate the whole orange. It was so delicious! I was so happy!

Games and Apples

Another memory I have is on rainy days Maggie and I would be playing Little Red Riding Hood in the corner of our kitchen. We built a little house (not a real one but just an imaginary one that was so real to us) with chairs, a little table, a blanket, some plates, all what we thought would be in Little Red Riding Hood's house. We would go in and out of it all day. Our father used to sit in his rocking chair in front of the fireplace smoking his pipe. We would catch him looking at us, and he always had the kindest look on his face, a little smile. Maggie and I used to love these days when we had him all to ourselves. All the others were outdoors or had gone to town. Sometimes we would hide from each other. Then we would ask our father "where did she go?" or "where was she hiding?" and he would look around but he would never tell on either one of us. He would say things like "maybe she went to the bedroom" or "maybe she went to the barn," but he would never really say where we went. This would continue for hours. It was our time together — just us.

Sometimes things got real bad and there was a shortage of food. Everyday everyone had chores to do. My sister would give Maggie and me a pocketbook and send us out to collect berries, apples, or anything edible we could find. We spent most of the day going around to all the other farms to collect our goodies without anyone seeing us. I was the youngest and smallest and could get under the fences easily, but poor Maggie who was bigger would get all scrapes and scratches trying to get under. One time we came home without a full bag, and my sister got mad, and we were sent back out again to get more or until the pocketbook was full.

My sister Lily told me that she and our cousin Madelyn would also try and get fruit from the neighbors. She said the two of them climbed up a tree and had all kinds of apples shoved into their blouses and skirts when they heard a noise. They looked down and saw an old man coming out of his farmhouse with a shotgun in his hand. He yelled up to them in the tree that if they didn't come down he was going to shoot them. Lily said they both flew down from the tree — all kinds of apples billowing out of their blouses, and when they reached the ground they held onto everything and started running. They did escape but they never went back to that farm again.

Gifts from America

There were packages that came from America. When the packages would arrive, my older cousins would come over to our house. We would all look over everything and take the clothes that fit each one of us — we were so happy and excited to get any item we could. I remember getting a cloth doll. It was the only one I ever had. I loved her and took her everywhere with me. I always played with her and took her to bed. She had a little pink dress on and blond hair, and I will always remember her. When I came to America I had to leave her behind because there was no room in my bag for her. I do remember crying that day, and I hid her under the sheets in my bed so she would be safe until I came back home. Later, I was told the only luggage I had with me was a small pocketbook with a Hershey bar and some small candies in it. I was told that inside my coat and Maggie's was a scapula my father had pinned to the lining of our coats for our safe keeping. I can't imagine how he felt doing that when we left.

Warmth of Happiness

When I look back at old pictures I can see Nellie, Terry, and Winnie with nice warm sweaters on, Maggie in a buttoned down coat and hat, Noel in his britches, and me in my fur coat! That was really warm. But when I look down at our feet we had no shoes on — Noel never wore long pants. Our feet were never cold. We used to go out and play in the snow in bare feet and never felt it.

Starting at the top: Terry, Nellie, Winnie. Maggie and Noel are on both sides of me in the front. It was a day we received clothes from America.

Swing to Remember

One time, my brother Noel, my cousin Vincent, sister Maggie, and I were up in the barn playing with a rope that we had made a swing out of. We played and enjoyed the swing for days. But this one day, they put me on the swing, and I still remember them saying, "Let's give her one more push for good luck!" Well they did, and I went flying through the air and landed in a bed of hay with a loud crack! My brother and Vincent got so scared they ran away to the woods and hid because they knew they were in trouble. My sister, Maggie, put me on her shoulders and carried me all the way down the hill to our house. The bone had almost come straight through my leg. They laid me on the kitchen floor near the fireplace where I could be warm. I remember my sisters leaning over me and covering me with blankets. My father got the horse and buggy. The buggy was wide open in the back, so it was very cold. Pakie carried me from the house and put me in the back of the buggy. Then he put clothes, blankets, and anything he and my family could find to keep me warm for the long, 7-mile trip to Boyle Hospital. He put his arms around me and stayed in the back with me until we arrived. I stayed in the hospital by myself for months because that was the year Ireland had its worst snowstorm in history. The year was 1947. They couldn't get me home, and they couldn't come visit me because of the snow. They said it probably saved my life! I remember in the hospital they kept both my legs in casts raised high, so one leg wouldn't grow faster than the other. I was like that for a long time. For some reason I don't remember much of my stay at the hospital. I just blocked it out. Because I was there for such a long time I think my guardian angel was with me and protected me so I wouldn't remember. My sister Winnie told me later that, back home, the snow was all the way up to the roof of our house, and it took days to shovel a tunnel to get out; supplies were starting to run short, and they needed water and firewood badly. At least by keeping me in the hospital, I was safe, kept warm, and fed.

When I came home, everyone was there waiting for me. All the neighbors, which were mostly my cousins, and said, "Aw, go on now. She'll be fit as a fiddle." I was six years old then, and when I walked my one leg used to swing out to the side. They think it was all because of the time I spent in traction. One of the neighbors used to come to my house every day and *make* me walk up and down the kitchen floor. Every time my leg swung out, he would hit it with a stick. I would yell like a banshee, and he would make me keep going! I remember swinging it myself because for some reason I thought it looked like I was dancing. It took a long time but his persistence really worked and after a while I was able to walk straight!

Another thing in my kitchen — they would get the meat from boxes that were stored next to the house and then sometimes they would hang the meat on the kitchen wall with hooks. The next day my sisters would slice it and make eggs with bacon and we would use that meat all week long. Sometimes right after a pig was slaughtered, the bladder was washed and cleaned and blown into a ball. Noel, Maggie, and I were given the ball, and we would run to get Vincent and the four of us would play catch and kickball. We would play for hours, throwing the ball back and forth to each other and have a great time. Back then on our farm we would have to think of games to play, make our own toys, or do without.

*I have my doll, and Maggie, Noel, and I had been
playing out in the fields without shoes on.*

Oh Halloween

On Halloween, we would all go in the woods at night with all of the other farmers and have a big bonfire to celebrate that the crops were all in and that we had enough food to last the winter. Everyone would dance, drink, and there would always be music. It lasted all night. I remember my older sisters dancing around the fire. They said there were fairies there dancing with the music also. Their hair was long, and it used to swing out and they looked so beautiful. I wanted to be like them.

At the School House

There was a time when we would all walk to school. We would go out the back door to the fields and follow a path to the bridge, which we would cross to get to our school, Clooncunny School, built in 1894. The school had two rooms. One room was big where we were all taught. The other was the teacher's room. We had bleacher seats that went from kindergarten to eighth grade. Each grade had its own bench. The younger kids were on the first bench, and my older brother and sisters were on the other benches above me. As we finished one grade, we moved to the next bench. The teacher would work with one grade at a time. The other grades would have to study or work with any assignments they got. We only had one teacher, so he must have had his hands full.

Our first trip back to Ireland. This was the old school house, and I still have an old ink well from there.

The old school house (Clooncunny School House) is still standing. It was built in 1894.

Johnnie and I are at the school house.

Nellie, me, and Johnnie (Pakie's only son) in front of the schoolhouse.

Farm Chores

There were always animals around our farm. Chickens, cats, goats, cows, and our dog Daisy. She had one blue eye and one brown eye. Daisy was Pakie's dog. She followed him everywhere and never left his side. One time, we were all in the kitchen and she started foaming at the mouth and running around in circles. My sister Nellie who was making dinner jumped up on the table and started screaming. Then we all jumped up there with her — all screaming — and held hands. Finally, my brother Pakie came running in and took the dog out of the house. We looked out the window and the dog was running around the house in circles. Finally she stopped, kept panting — then lay down and eventually went to sleep. Sometimes this happens to some dogs. After that she was fine, and it never happened again. She was lucky because sometimes if there were too many animals overrunning the farm, or if they got too sickly, they were taken to the lake and drowned. This used to happen quite often.

A few days later Nellie, Winnie, and Terry were out doing chores on the farm. They were milking the cows and feeding the chickens. Then Nellie remembered she had to get water from the well to boil water for dinner. The well was near a bog (which is water filled with dirt) where we got the peat to heat our house. She was running so fast she tripped and fell into the well. She slowly sank down and was yelling for help. Winnie and Terry came running, and they said by the time they got there they saw her dress had billowed out and there was only one finger sticking out of the water. They grabbed her hand and pulled her up. They said the dress saved her life because it kept her afloat. Later we would kid around and say, "Oh, here comes Nell in the well." She was so lucky that day.

Loving to Laugh

My brother Noel used to play all day with Vincent. Maggie and I used to try and follow them but they would always hide on us. They were inseparable. Noel told me one day they went to visit our aunt and uncle. On the way home there was an old lady on another farm and she called them over. They said she seemed a little crazy. She was making butter in the churn on a very warm day. There were flies in it — and it was all curdled up. They tried to run away, but she caught them and told them they would really like it. She forced them to eat it and both of them got sick. Noel said to this day he could never eat butter again. Another day Maggie and I were following Noel and Vincent around, and we found them next to the barn.

They didn't see us so we kept hiding and looking out of the bushes to see what they were doing. Finally we heard them laughing and when we came over to see, they were playing a game of "who could pee the farthest" to hit the barn wall. Well we started laughing and giggling, and they heard us so we ran down to the fields and hid. We could hear them in the distance yelling at us, but we kept running and we never did get caught!

Our cousin Vincent still lives in Ireland. He has a beautiful house and a large farm. Every so often he would come to visit America and stay awhile, but he always went back home. We still have a good laugh when we talk about all those times we spent together as kids.

Breaking up the Family

One of the saddest days was when we were told to come outside. We were lined up by age. Our aunt and uncle were there from Cavan to pick one of us to come live with them to help my father. They picked my sister Attracta because she was the same age as their daughter. They took her home to live with them in Cavan. As children we didn't understand that my father was very sick and couldn't take care of all of us. Attracta grew up with our cousins, went through school and became a nurse in England. She later came to American where she met her husband, had children, and built a wonderful life.

As time went by my father got sicker, and knew he needed to get help with the children. He went to the convent and asked if they could help by taking some of the younger ones but for some reason they couldn't. We never found out why. Maybe because he owned a farm. We don't know. He couldn't read or write, but he sent word to his family in America to please help him and take some of the children there.

Nellie (in the middle) and our two cousins on each side are standing, and Maggie, Terry, and I are sitting in a horse and buggy.

Off to America

The first to go to America was my oldest sister Lily. She was 18 at the time. She went to Dublin and then to Cork, where she got on a boat. The boat was a converted troop ship from the war. It was supposed to take 10 days but it took another five days because it had to get around a fierce storm. Everyone had to stay below deck — nobody could go up on deck. They slept in the same bunk beds that the sailors slept in during the war. The bunk beds were shifting all night along with the boat. She said she got sea sick a few times and an older woman she had met on the dock was in the bunk below her — they talked the whole trip, and she would always bring Lily something to eat. She was so kind. Lily was picked up when they landed at

Ellis Island by my Aunt Ellen and Uncle Jerome. She went to live at my Aunt Ellen, Uncle Jerome, and their daughter Sheila's house in Caldwell, New Jersey. She got a job there, met her husband, married and had five children.

I am on the left with Lily and Maggie the first year we came to America. We went to visit Lily and this picture was taken.

Next to go were Maggie and I. I was 9, and Maggie was 10 years old. They told us we were going on a two-week holiday so we were happy!! Before we left, everyone was standing outside our front door and we kissed them all goodbye. My father's head was bent down, and he gave me a long hug and was shaking. He didn't want me to see him cry. They were all saying their "goodbyes" to us except Pakie, who was 17 at the time. Later, I found out that he went into the woods and stayed there all night and didn't come home until the next day because he knew *he would never see us again*!

We went and stayed with our cousins in Dublin until it was time for us to leave Ireland. They had one of the biggest houses I had ever seen. Their living room was huge with a big fireplace. They had a large kitchen with a sink, and my cousin had to show me what to do when I went to the bathroom because I had never seen a toilet before. She told me when I was finished I had to pull a long rope down — so I did, and it made a loud swishing sound — I jumped back — it scared me to death. Then I looked to the side and saw a sink with running water to wash my hands, also a bathtub (I was told these names later). I had never seen anything like this — it was a miracle! Then we had a delicious dinner. I could hardly reach the table it was so huge. Soon after that, it was time for bed. We changed our clothes and had such a hard time getting up into the bed. It was so big! It had four posts (which we thought were sticks or logs) and a huge backboard all carved. Finally we made it into the bed, got under the covers, and were just looking around the room. We couldn't believe it; we had never seen a bed that big before. All of a sudden the bedroom door opened and our cousin came into our room. She just smiled at us and said, "I thought it would be good for you girls if I sleep with you tonight because you might be afraid or lonely." She was very sweet and kind but Maggie and I were afraid of new people. "No we're OK," we both said together. She walked over to the bed and gave us a kiss on the forehead and said, "good night." Finally, we went to sleep. I often wonder what she must have thought of us two strange girls.

The next day we were taken to the airport where the plane was waiting for us. We had to climb up the outside stairs to get into the plane. Once inside, a stewardess told us where to sit, and I think she kept an eye on us because she knew we were all alone. Back then we didn't need an adult with us to fly. I was looking out the window and already getting lonesome for my father and family. As the plane rose I could see all the farms and the green grass. I could see the cows on the hillside and the beautiful lakes in the distance, but then I thought we were going on a great holiday and would be back shortly. We weren't unhappy or afraid.

I am with Maggie out in the fields. Lily actually made Maggie's dress, and she remembers sewing the flowers on it.

Our plane was a twin-engine plane that landed in Gander, Newfoundland, to refuel. I got sick and Maggie took care of me. She found me a place to sit and went to get some orange juice. She had to go to the bathroom, so she told me to stay there, which I did. She was gone for a while, and she must have gotten lost because later she was found walking up the steps to get back on the plane — only it was a Russian airplane! Thank God for the stewardess who found her and put her back on the right plane.

When we arrived in America, we went to my Aunt Annie's (my father's sister who was also born in Ireland and came to America as a young girl) and Uncle Joe's house. They met while working for Thomas Edison who lived on an Estate in Llewelyn Park, New Jersey. She was the maid, and he was the butler. They eventually got married and bought their house on Eagle Rock Avenue, right across the street from Llewellyn Park, where they had worked. Living there also was her daughter, Betty Ferraer, her husband, Freddie, and their two daughters, Ellen and Betty-Ann. Betty Ann and Ellen became like two other sisters to me also. We were all raised the same — what one got the other got — and Ellen and I were always dressed alike, especially for our communions and confirmations.

Aunt Annie's house was a big house, and there were a lot of people visiting there and sometimes staying there. The day we arrived, Maggie and I never left each other's side. We didn't know who these people were, and we were both for the first time a little afraid. Finally, our cousin told Maggie she was going home with them that day to live in their house in Bloomfield, New Jersey. They had two sons and had just lost their daughter from drowning, so they wanted a girl. I remember standing on the front porch watching her go in their car, and I didn't really understand where she was going and why they were taking her away from me. I felt so alone standing there, but I was told to come inside because it was getting cold out and I might catch a cold.

The first night at my house I was put in a bed with Betty's daughter Ellen because we were the same age (only four days apart). Betty Ann, Ellen's sister, was little so she was in a crib. The next morning when we woke up, Ellen kept scratching her head. We found out I had cooties, and I never knew it. I never felt a thing. I wonder if the people on the plane ever caught the cooties. How could I never have felt them? I was probably used to it. Well, the next day Ellen and I were put in the bathtub and with one of those thin sharp combs and some ointment, the problem was solved. To this day, we say that must have been the day we bonded.

I didn't see Maggie again for about six months, but when I did we were so glad to see each other, and we had so much fun together. When we were sent to bed we hid under the covers and played games. Sometimes we would cry a little, but then we both knew we had to be brave and not let anyone else see us cry. Sometimes we would use the flashlight so we could read little books or tell each other stories of what was happening at each other's house. This could go on for a long time, and finally we would go to sleep.

Every night her Mom and Dad used to say the rosary in bed. It would start out in their room very loudly. Hail Mary full of grace, and then to the two sons Matt and Tommy's rooms — the

Lord will be with thee — the first decade of rosary — then Maggie and I would do the third with all of us praying out loud and finish the last Amen. When it used to come to our turn it was so hard for us not to giggle and look at each other because we had never done anything like that before. Eventually, we got used to it, and it went pretty fast. My time staying with her went quickly, and then it was time for me to go back to West Orange.

Back in West Orange, I would wonder why I was here. Ireland was so far away that I thought it was best not to think of it again. That kept me going. Back then you didn't ask anyone questions; you just kept going and tried to do the best you could.

Maggie eventually graduated high school, graduated college, and became a teacher. She got married and has two grown children and two grandchildren.

Magazines in the Mail

As I grew up in my Aunt Annie's house, there was Betty's husband, Freddie. Everyone loved him, as much as they did Betty. I remember him always playing the harmonica. When we got a little older, there was always a hayride, and all the kids went on it. They needed a chaperone so Freddie was chosen. He was so good and liked by everyone. We didn't do anything bad on the hayride, but if we had he would never have told on us. One time, I was at church, and they were selling subscriptions to a magazine, so I subscribed, thinking it would be something good to read. Little did I know that soon after the magazine started coming to our house everyone was questioned about who ordered the magazine. We were getting billed and had to start making payments. When it was my turn, I said that I had no idea, and I said I didn't order the magazines. I wasn't going to back down, so then they sent me out to the kitchen to see Freddie (or Daddy as I was now calling him). He told me to sit down, which I did, and he held one of my hands and looked right at me and said, "Did you sign up for those magazines?" Immediately, I said "yes." I don't know why, but I knew I could trust him, and I knew he would protect me and I wouldn't get a spanking. Soon after, the problem was solved, and we didn't get any more magazines.

Another time, he took Ellen and me up the hill to visit some people he worked with. When we got there, they told us to sit in the living room and watch TV, and then they went into the kitchen with Freddie. Ellen and I didn't like them. A while later, I could hear them talking, and the woman said, "Is that the little girl you brought from Ireland?" He said "yes" and the woman said, "Well, if you don't want her or she's too much trouble, we could always adopt her from you." I heard a fist hit the kitchen table and Freddie saying, "That's my daughter, and no one is taking her from me." With that, he came out of the kitchen and told Ellen and me, "Let's go. We're out of here!!" We left, and we never went back there again.

Best Friends

After arriving here, I went to Our Lady of Lourdes Grammar School where they placed me in the second grade. I was left-handed but the nuns made me write with my right hand, which was the way they did it in those days. I remember writing circles with my right hand, and eventually I got the hang of it. To this day however all my strength is in my left hand. In front of the church there was a wall about four feet high. When we would get out of class we would be standing near it. I went up on the grass and would yell, "Ready or not, here I come!!" and I would run fast, spread my arms out, and jump off the wall and all the kids would catch me, and I would say, "Do it again." I had no fear, but the nuns saw all of us and told the kids: "The next time Christina does that don't catch her and then she'll stop doing it!" Thank God for my little friends. They told me in secret, and we didn't do it again. The nun probably saved me from getting killed.

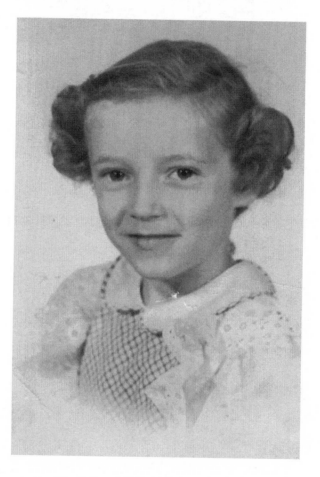

My first school picture taken when I came to America. I was put in the 2nd grade. I was 9 years old.

One of my classmates told me recently that when I came to West Orange, the first day she saw me was in the back of Our Lady of Lourdes Church. She said I was standing by myself looking so bewildered to see where to go and what I should do next. She said the sun was shining brightly into the church. The breeze and wind blew my hair all wild — and she said she thought I was a little angel! We are best friends to this day, and now we both know better!!

Betty and Freddie

*I am with BettyAnn, Freddie, Cousin Tommy,
and Ellen at the Jersey Shore.*

Years later, I remember Freddie babysitting for me. I had three sons by that time. He loved coming to our house and always called the boys "the hard chargers." One afternoon, we were going to a wedding, and I said, "Now Daddy, I don't want the boys going out after we leave." He would always say, "No problem." A long time later, we found out from the boys that after we left he would give them each money and let them go to Friendly's to get ice cream as long as they didn't tell us. They told me they had ice cream and came <u>right</u> <u>home</u>. Then I said, "Oh really?" and then they all looked at each other and had a <u>little</u> <u>smile</u>, so I didn't push it further.

Lessons to Learn

I will never forget playing hopscotch with the kids on the block. I would take my shoes off. The kids would say, "Aren't your feet cold?" and of course I would say "no." Then it popped into my head that I was going to show them something. I went back to my house and got a needle and thread and came back to the kids. I sat down on the sidewalk and told them to come look. I took the needle and sewed one of my toes to the other. They were screaming and saying, "OH NO, STOP!" They must have thought I was crazy. What they didn't realize was the calluses on my feet were so thick I couldn't feel a thing! Well, I got into some trouble for doing that, and I never did it again. There were a lot more lessons I had to learn in America.

Father Passes

I was here a year when my father died. He died of stomach cancer. He was 59 years old. I remember playing in the playground at Our Lady of Lourdes Grammar School when a nun came over and called me. She took me aside and told me "There's something I have to tell you" — and I said "yes?" And then she said, "Your father died today. Say a prayer," which I did with her, and then she just walked away — the recess bell rang, and we were told to go back to the classroom — recess was over. I stood there and didn't know what to do. All the kids were going back to class, so I went back with them. That night I remember lying in bed (all by myself), and I kept thinking about my father and how alone I felt for the first time and didn't know what was going to happen to me. Then I thought of my mother, but I couldn't see her because I was too young when she died, and I don't remember her face. There was no picture of her. Back then, there weren't many pictures taken. But the longer I lay there I started praying to God to help me, and I prayed so hard (this sounds crazy) in the darkness I saw Jesus' face, and I knew from that day on I was going to be okay, and I was going to be strong no matter what happened to me.

Back at Home

My brother, Noel, was the next to come. He was 12 years old. Noel remembers Pakie and our father taking him to Boyle to catch the train to Dublin. While Noel was on the train, my father stood with his arms crossed and watched the train slowly taking Noel away while Pakie ran along the side of the train not wanting Noel to go. Both he and my father were crying. Noel stuck his head out the window and waved good-bye. He was thinking like I did that he was going on a holiday.

Noel made it to Dublin and was kept there for a week. There was some problem with his papers. So until it was resolved he was allowed to go back home. When he got back to the farm he said it was so quiet so he went looking around.

He found Pakie out in the field, and when Pakie turned around and saw Noel. He couldn't believe it. Pakie said in shock, "What are you doing here?" and Noel replied, "There was a delay so they sent me back here until all the paperwork was ready." Well, Pakie's face lit up, and he went over and gave Noel a big hug, and tears welled up in his eyes. Noel hugged back and said, "What are you crying about?! You thought you'd get rid of me that fast!?" After a while of hugging, Pakie said, "Can ye come now and help me milk the cows?" Noel said, "sure," and off they went.

While there, my father went to the hospital and they would go visit him often. Two weeks later he died. Noel was so happy he could be with him one last time. Word was sent that all of Noel's papers were finished so he was sent back to Dublin a second time and then to the United States. I was so happy he came to live with me in our house.

I felt so protected and I knew he would always take care of me. In our house on Eagle Rock Ave., West Orange we had a big attic, and that is where we all slept. Noel was always playing tricks. We would all go to sleep not knowing he was hiding under the bed. Then he would jump out and we'd all scream.

He was 12 years old when he came, and Betty would take us all down to Bamberger's in Newark to sit on Santa's lap. At first, he refused saying he was too old but then we all coached him and finally he did. We all had our picture taken on Santa's lap. Years later, I asked him where his picture of Santa was. He had this sneaky little grin on his face. He told me he found it, and it just happened to disappear!

Another night, he was reading a medical magazine. The next day before we got up for school, we went over to wake Noel up. He said he couldn't move. We thought he was kidding around so we went downstairs. Later, we heard him yelling, "Betty, I have polio." Mommy ran up the stairs, and she couldn't get him up. She sent us off to school and then called the doctor. He came to the house; that was when doctors made house calls.

He checked Noel and then saw the magazine. He asked, "Were you reading this right before you went to sleep?" Noel said, "Yes." The doctor then made Noel lift both legs, sit on the side of the bed, put his feet on the floor, and stand up. Well, he did stand up and the doctor told him to walk across the floor, which he was able to do, and that was the end of the polio!!

Betty Ann now owns the same house, and whenever I go visit I always think of the fun times we had. Our house was always the place to go to have parties. All of Ellen's friends, my friends, and of course Noel's friends used to come. Freddie was the chaperone. He would always be there (the parties were usually in the basement) and we had rock and roll music on. It was a great way to get together and have fun. Sometimes the party would get a little bit rowdy and Mommy would come down the cellar stairs with a broom. The house had an opening where we could go out the back way by going up the stairs and opening two doors. They swung open. Well, when everyone heard her coming, they flew out of the basement. She caught a few of the boys, but most got away. One boy was running around the front yard, and she was chasing him with the broom, but he got away. Another boy was on the chaise lounge in our backyard under a tree with a girl. Well, she grabbed the lounge and turned it over. They went flying and then they both ran away through the neighbors' yards. He turned out to be none other than the boy from the bogs of Ireland — I won't say his name! Looking back, it never bothered our friends, and they would always come back to our house with their heads down and say, "Hi Betty. We won't do that again." She would say, "I know. Now come on in and join the rest of the gang in the basement." She knew all of their parents and where they lived. They were all good kids. Years later, the boys she was chasing with a broom turned out to be a judge, a lawyer, and a business owner. They all turned out to be good and hard-working young men.

One day we were going to high school, and Noel had his first car. Ellen and I asked him if he would drive us (it was pretty far — we would have to take the bus if he didn't). He said yes, but when we got to the school, he made us scoot down in the back seat because he didn't want any of his friends seeing him drive his sisters to school. We did what we were told, and no one ever knew, so he didn't get teased.

Voyage Crossing

The next to come to America were my two sisters Nellie and Terry and my other sister Winnie. Now Pakie was the only one left on the farm. He and Vincent would share the chores and help each other caring for the cattle. They were able to sell their cattle on the market and have continued to be very successful. Nellie and Terry also came over on a ship — they were all huddled down in the lower quarters with all the other immigrants from all over. Every night the music would start and everyone started dancing. It didn't matter what nationality anyone was. Nellie danced all night! Terry told me she would stay in her top bunk while all this was going on. She was so afraid for anyone to see her because when she was young she had polio in one of her legs and developed a limp. She was afraid someone would see her and she would be reported. She could do everything else with no problem, but it was hard for her to dance. The trip over was very long and tedious and before they arrived Terry was terrified because they were told that sometimes when people arrived at Ellis Island they might get rejected and sent back to their homes because of certain illnesses. She said after they got off the ship they had to wait on really long lines that took hours. Thank God she was approved, and she and Nellie came to live in our house in West Orange. They both got good jobs and eventually moved into their own apartment.

When Winnie came to America she lived with my Aunt Betty and Uncle Pat in Far Hills, New Jersey. Aunt Betty suffered a few miscarriages and was thrilled to have Winnie come live with her. She was a lovely, gentle woman. She would light up when anyone came to visit. They lived on a farm where they would grow their own vegetables and other produce. They raised chickens. I used to go spend some time in the summer with Winnie. Uncle Pat used to read our tea leaves from the cups after we had tea. He would always start out by saying — "from what I can see here — you're going to receive a letter." He would say that to all of us. I remember Aunt Betty used to come up to Winnie's bedroom and she would have strips of cloth that she would curl Winnie's hair and then mine. I felt so grown up when the next day she would take the ribbons out and we would have nice, curly hair.

Killing Chickens

Sometimes when we would walk by the barn we could see Uncle Pat with a chicken on a board where he was getting ready to chop its head off. Then we would hear a whack and knew it was over. He would then hang the chicken upside down in the barn to drain all the blood out. The next night that is what we had for dinner. Ellen always remembers going there with me and when we sat for dinner our mashed potatoes would always have a raw egg in the middle of it. We would try to eat around it but could not eat that egg. Then, every day he would make us sniff detergent up our noses — me, Ellen, and Winnie would just keep sneezing — he said it was good because it got rid of all the germs we had. We had to say, it did clear up our head colds.

Winnie's Watch

I remember when Winnie graduated she got a beautiful watch. She put the watch on her right arm going up the aisle so everyone could see it on the right hand side. Then, she when she got up to the alter, she went to the left side and changed the watch to her left arm so people could see it when she was coming down the left hand side. She was so proud of her beautiful watch that she wore it every day.

She eventually moved in with my two sisters and got a job at the bank. The three of them had so much fun living together. They used to love going to McGoverns in Newark to have fun. All of the Irish people went there. They were always laughing, dancing, having a few refreshments, and enjoying a jolly good time. I was about 18, and I was their designated driver. It worked out well, and we all got home safe and sound. Plus, I could stay at their apartment and hear all the good stories.

Eventually they all met their spouses, got married, and had children.

A Shore Summer

When I was going into my sophomore year in high school, I got a job working down the shore just for the summer as a babysitter and a housekeeper. I thought I was going to be mostly babysitting, but when I got there it was totally different. My job was doing the chores and maybe only three times babysitting. I was told I couldn't eat with the family, and I had to eat in the kitchen. Before I ate breakfast the owner of the house would come to my room, knock, and always say "rise and shine" that was 7 a.m. She then took me downstairs to her husbands' office, and that was the first room I had to clean, then I could have my breakfast. The kids went to camp. So my day began. I would start in the kitchen, do the dishes, sweep and mop the floor, make sure everything was shiny. Next was the living room and dining room. It was a big house, and I just cleaned all day. Upstairs I had to make all the beds, clean the kids' rooms, vacuum, and dust, and finally I would be finished around 3 and then she would let me go to the public pool.

I only had two big problems at my babysitting and house-cleaning job. One was when they were having a big party at their house. She had me staying home for days — polishing the silver — then using a cloth to make it shine — buffing it. That took hours. Next making sure all the Waterford Crystal was washed and shining. She was having it catered so I was allowed out that night.

The next day the kitchen had to be cleaned so I started with the glasses and all of a sudden I heard a crack!!! I looked down at my hands and there was the beautiful Waterford Crystal glass broken in half. I couldn't believe it — then I thought what am I going to do — so I thought real quick, went over to the garbage and wrapped the glass in a paper towel and put it at the bottom of the can and put all the other garbage on top of it.

That afternoon I went to the pool and had a great time. When I got home she was sitting on the porch (which I never have seen her do before) she said, "Is there something you want to tell me?" I said "no" with a quizzical look on my face — then she put her hand behind her back and took something out — it was the broken wine glass. I just looked at her and said to myself — I'm dead! I said, "I am sorry. I didn't mean to do it. It was an accident, and I was afraid to tell you." She got up and said, "Don't ever do anything like that again because I will always know."

Another time and, thank God, the last time I got in trouble — she used to always make me go down the cellar — I was only 15 — and do all the ironing. I would spend the whole day down there. One item I remember was one of her dresses that had pleats on the bottom. I tried every which way to iron it. Finally I laid the skirt part out and started ironing from the bottom up. When I was finished it was all billowed out. I thought it looked good. Well when she came home she went downstairs to check on my ironing. I used to hang everything up. I could hear a curse word and then a yell — Christina come down here. I did and she was holding the dress. What have you done — you ruined my dress — again I said I am sorry — then she put the dress back on the ironing board and showed me how to do pleats. I must have been down there three hours on that dress. Finally she came down and checked me and said it was okay. From that day forward she would never let me iron any of her dresses again. Boy, was I glad! (I was getting $15 a week!)

A Sweet Beginning

Every day I would go up to the pool and sit by myself and read a book. I was lonely for my friends back home. One day a couple of kids came over and asked me my name and where did I live. They said they had seen me sitting by myself. I told them, and they said they knew who I was living with. They asked me to come to a party, and I said I would have to find out. I went home to the house, and she said I could go as long as they came to the house to pick me up and bring me home. Well they did, and everything went fine. It made my whole summer go by so much faster. They turned out to be my good friends, and after I got home to West Orange, two girls came up and stayed with me. Thank God for meeting those kids.

We would all meet at 16th Avenue in Belmar, and that was the first time I saw Dick. I thought he was so handsome; he was wearing an Immaculate High School jacket and peg pants. He had a great smile. Unfortunately he was with someone (a beautiful girl), and I thought to myself that it was the end for me. We did keep looking at each other and said "hello" but that was it. We all went to a beach party, and I kept looking for him but he was gone. I thought that was the last time I'd ever see him again. The summer ended, and we all went back to school and our normal lives.

I went back home, back to school to my sophomore year, and one day I was sitting in a booth in a store called the Kandy Kane. Everyone used to go there after school to hang out. The kids were from different towns but mostly West Orange. The owner, John Boylan, came over to our table and said "Chris could I see you for a moment?" I said sure and when I walked over to him he said — "Would you like to work here in the Kandy Kane after school? You would just have to make milkshakes, sodas, ice cream, hamburgers, etc.). I said yes right away and was honored to be chosen out of everyone for the job.

I worked there throughout my years in high school and loved it. It wasn't like a job because all my friends came in every day after school to hang out. Sometimes when it was slow he asked me if I would go upstairs and babysit because that's where his family lived. At the time there were 5 children — I used to love going upstairs to babysit; his wife Mary was so nice and the kids were so cute.

Soon after John moved the family to a home at the top of the hill in West Orange. Time went by and I dated other guys — I even went steady with a boy who gave me a ring that I would hang around my neck — that's what we did; it meant we were going steady.

Then one day I looked up over the soda counter and who was sitting there but Dick and his friend Timmy Farrell. There I was with the same feeling again. I could hardly breathe. And we actually started talking. I didn't ask him anything about who he was going with but when I was finished with my shift, we sat in one of the booths. Tim had gone by then so we were able to talk. He was so easy to be with. Then I decided to take a chance and I asked him to come to my high school's friend's Sweet Sixteen Party. He said yes, and I was shocked! We went to the party and had a great time. Then he asked me if I would go out with him again. I said sure. Some time went by, he called and asked if I wanted to go to the drive-in movies with him. Of course I said yes, and that was the real beginning of our dating.

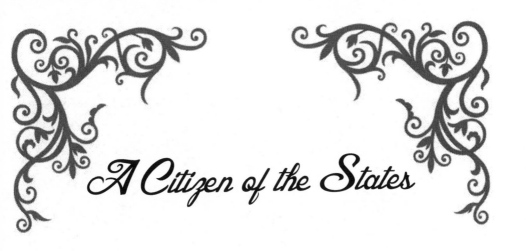

A Citizen of the States

When I graduated from high school, I knew I had to now become a citizen of the United States. So I went to the town hall myself, and there was a large questionnaire you had to fill out, which I did. Then one of the clerks asked me several questions — one was, "If the United States and Ireland got into a war, who would you back?" I really didn't know what to say. In my head I was thinking, oh my God, I don't want them to do anything to Ireland — because my brother and family were still there, and I still loved Ireland so much, but then I got myself together and realized what he asked, and then I said, "the United States" because I loved this country as much as my own for all the great things it had given me.

My high school graduation picture.

Story of Love

Dick and I got engaged on my Aunt's front porch and when he gave me the ring, we both teared up. I said "it's beautiful," and then right away without waiting I said, "How about if we get married in September?" He said sure, and that was it. We both didn't want to wait too long! I was 19 he was 21.

We got married in Our Lady of Lourdes Church, in West Orange. In the wedding party were my sister Maggie, my two sisters Betty Ann and Ellen, Dick's twin sister Ellen, and my best friend Pam; the groomsmen were Dick's brother Charlie, my brother Noel, Jack McMorrow, Tim Farrell, and Evan Cahill. The church was packed, and Daddy (Freddie) gave me away. When the ceremony was over we walked out the front doors of the Church, and we could hear cheering and wishing us good luck! When we looked across the street, we saw the gang from the Kandy Kane cheering — because the building was right across the street from the Church.

Our wedding day! September 23, 1961

From left: Maggie, Terry, me, Nellie, Winnie, Lily, and Noel at my wedding.

We had been married only three months when Dick got called into the Army. He served six months in Ft. Knox and the rest of the time in the National Guard. We first lived in East Orange in a one-bedroom apartment over a drug store. The Shop Rite building was right across the parking lot. There was a rope that went right across the lot so I would hang all our clothes across it. My oldest son Danny was born there, and I used to wash his diapers and hang them across the line. All of my neighbors also did this. There were no diaper pick-up services at that time. The rent was $65 a month, so that was very reasonable. I will always remember when Maggie and her boyfriend Marty came to visit us. We never realized how hot the apartment was because we were so used to it. Well a few days later there was a knock on the door and when we opened it there was a big box with a window air conditioner in it. Dick hooked it up, and we couldn't believe the difference. At that time we didn't have money to get our own. We were so glad how thoughtful they were, and I will always be grateful. After two years of living there we moved to Livingston, and that's where Timmy and Craig were born. They all went to school there. About five years before Dick retired we moved to the Shore, and that is where I've lived ever since.

I am next to Dick, and from the left: Danny, Craig, and Timmy. The first year we moved to our new house in Livingston, New Jersey. Craig was just born. Tim was 3, and Danny was 5.

Lessons to Learn

In our house growing up, every Sunday Aunt Annie always had our aunts, uncles, and cousins to dinner. It was a ritual, and we all had to be there. After dinner, the aunts would sit in the living room and the men would continue to sit and talk at the dining room table. Whenever they would come to visit, they would simply shake your hand to say hello. I always remember thinking they seemed so stiff, never smiling or laughing, except for Aunt Catherine, my father's sister. She would always have her six-pack of beer next to her chair. Aunt Catherine and Uncle Johnnie would never leave until the show "Lassie" was over. In the meantime, Uncle Johnnie would let Noel use his car that whole afternoon, but he had to always get it back before the end of the show. Noel always did get the car back in time, and Aunt Catherine never found out.

Years later, Noel met Dottie, a fine Italian girl, and they started going steady. One Sunday, he brought her to our house for dinner, and when she came in she went right up to all of the aunts and cousins and gave them a big kiss on the cheek along with a big hug. Well, they all stiffened up!! There was such a look of shock on their faces that they had been kissed. That night I asked Aunt Annie why they were so afraid of being kissed, and she told me that they had just gotten word from Ireland that one of the cousin's babies had died. A visitor had kissed the baby on the lips, and they found out later he had consumption. They were always brought up to never kiss because you never knew who might have the sickness.

Well, time went by, and Dottie came every Sunday, and they got so used to her kissing them on the cheek. When she didn't come on occasion, they really missed her warmth and affection. As time went by, everyone loosened up and the stiffness left their bodies and they would let us kiss their cheeks. What I thought was cold people was only what they had learned and what information they were brought up with. By the time I got married and they met Dick (who hugged and loved everybody) at my wedding, they were all kissing and hugging each other!! All of us in the family thank Dottie for helping our family to get over their fears and to become more warm. I loved Dottie. She was more than Noel's wife. She was also like a sister and a best friend to me. Noel and Dottie got married and had two children and a grandson.

Back to Ireland

There were several times I went back to Ireland. The first time I went back I was 38 years old — a long time had passed and I didn't know what to expect. We were on a tour, and we broke away to go to Roscommon where we lived. The tour bus dropped us off (me, Dick, and Nellie), and we took another bus to get to the farm. Back in Ireland then there were no phones to call ahead, so while we were riding the bus a woman noticed Nellie from her childhood and came back to talk to us. She said she was getting off at the next stop and would have someone drive to Pakie's house to let him know we were on our way. When we arrived in Derry Cough, standing outside Mahon's store (still standing and doing business) was my brother Pakie, his wife Mary Francis, and their son Johnnie. I was afraid to get off the bus because I thought he wouldn't recognize me. I made Dick and Nellie go first and then when he saw me, the both of us started hugging. All of us were so happy to see each other and to be there. That evening we went to Harrington's Pub, and I think everyone who knew the Brennan Family was there. They all wanted to meet Pakie's sisters who were all grown up now. Once the music started we all got up and danced. Nellie and I were exhausted because when we sat down from dancing with one gentleman we were asked to dance by another one. Dick and Pakie were sitting next to each other just enjoying the fun.

Then it was time to leave the pub, so we walked down the road to Mary Francis' and Pakie's house. Not just us, but people from the pub. Mary Frances takes out all kinds of food that she had prepared that day. We all sat around the kitchen table eating. They had little sandwiches — we could either have a cheese sandwich or a ham sandwich — they never put both together. They had a potbelly stove but no gas heating, and we all talked most of the night. After everyone left, Mary Francis said to us — "Now will ye be wanting to go to the 9, 10, or 12 o'clock Mass tomorrow?" We thought we were going to pass out; we looked at each other and said together the 12 o'clock Mass would be fine! When we got into bed, there was no heat, so we were given a couple of hot water bottles and they worked fine.

The next morning we woke around 9 after going to bed around 4:30 a.m., and I had the worst headache — it must have been the delicious pints I was drinking. Then Dick and Nellie got up. When I went to get dressed, I was hysterical, I couldn't find my slip — I was looking all over the room — couldn't find it — I found the stockings, heels and dress because that's what people wore to church back then. As I was running around the room a cow stuck his head in the bedroom window, and I thought he possibly could have eaten it! So finally I gave up and said, "I just have to forget about my slip today" — so I lifted up my nightgown, and I heard Dick laughing. I looked down and there was my slip. I had forgotten to take it off the night before and just put my nightgown over it. Oh, I was so relieved!

My parents' headstone.

We also went to the graveyard, and I could not believe there was no headstone for my mother's grave, so when we got back home to America, I called all of my sisters and brother and asked if we should get a headstone. Right away they all said that of course we should, so we all chipped in. I ordered the new headstone, and the next time I went back, it was such a beautiful sight to see. It was made in the shape of a Celtic cross with both of my parents' names along with Uncle Jimmy's name engraved on it. The headstone stands at the top of the hill where we can almost see it as we come into the cemetery. Without the stone, we would never know exactly where our parents were buried unless we had someone to show us. It's one of the proudest moments in my life that we were able to do this for our parents.

We stayed in Ireland for about a week and had a wonderful time! Then it was time to go. In the meantime our tourist bus was going to meet us in the town to pick us up. It was a Sunday, and everything was closed, but all of Pakie's friends and neighbors got the bar owner and the police to open it up. Now I heard later that the people getting off the tour bus were mumbling and wondering what kind of place this was — they didn't want to stop there. It was around 2 in the afternoon, and they wanted to do some sightseeing — but they all came into the Pub got into the booths and then the beer started flowing, food started coming out of the kitchen, and a three-piece band started playing. Next thing you know they are all out dancing and having a ball. Even local people came in to enjoy themselves. They were all different nationalities there — most Americans, some Italians, and others. What a wonderful afternoon! Well, the bus driver said it was close to 7 p.m. so we had to go — but in the meantime Nellie and I took Pakie, Mary Frances, and Johnnie around to all the tables and introduced them and told them our story and then they understood why the bus stopped. I remember it like it was yesterday. When it was time to leave everyone got back on the bus and we were the last to leave. We knew from now on we would be back but that first good-bye as an adult was so hard. We all kissed and hugged, all crying — even little Johnnie — and we got back on the bus. When we started to walk to our seat

I couldn't lift my head up. I was crying and feeling so sad for Pakie. We were leaving him again. It broke my heart. Thank God he had such a wonderful wife and son to spend his life with. I sat next to the window, and we all waved goodbye. The most amazing thing was most of the whole bus was crying — an Italian woman was sobbing and tapped my hand and said "You're all going to be fine — may God be with you!"

The next few days we got back into the swing of things, got back on the bus, and went up to the Cliffs of Mohr. For you that don't know — the road leading to the cliffs is kind of on an angle — so I was sitting next to Nellie, who was sitting next to the window and she said, "Oh Chris, look at all the cows over on the hill have one leg shorter than the other" — so when I looked, I didn't know what to think because it looked that way to me too! Well, someone must have heard our conversation and then everyone started laughing. It turns out because of the slanted angle of the ground the cows had to walk with two legs higher than the other two, so it does look like they are on two legs! Nellie said,

"See, I was right!" That was a wonderful trip, and after that we did go back several more times making it easier and easier to say goodbye each time.

Pakie, Nellie, and I on our first trip back to Ireland after 29 years.

I am standing in the back of our house. Mostly everything was gone, but the walls were still standing.

Dick, Pakie, and I are in the local pub on our first trip back to Ireland.

Dick and I on our ride to a castle up the hill.

Mary Fraces, Johnnie, me, and Nellie on our first trip back. This store was still standing and operating in Derry Cough 29 years after I left Ireland.

This is the back door to our old house.

Dick and I are on the river on our first trip back to Ireland.

With the Boys

One of the last times I went back to Ireland I was with Dick and my three sons. (None of them were married, and they were all in their thirties.) We went to our farm and the house I was born in. The walls were still standing, but the roof was gone, and everything was all overgrown. After walking around the house and barn the boys stepped inside the house and looked around. Their first reaction was how could so many people have lived in such a small space? They were overwhelmed. The fireplace was still standing, and there was an old pot for boiling water still on the grate. We picked up some small stones and a few little bottles to take home with us. I still have them on my bookshelf and will never let them go. We went to the schoolhouse where we all went to school. It was still standing, and someone was storing a boat in there.

After that we went back walking in the fields and I could see Dick and Pakie talking to each other (I don't think that either one knew what the other was saying, because Pakie spoke so low and Dick couldn't hear.) The boys and I were laughing a little about that. As we were standing there I could see Pakie looking at Dick and the boys, and I know how proud he was. He knew my mother and father would have been happy to know I married a wonderful man and had three strong, caring, and loving Irish sons.

This is the Cliffs of Mohr.
From left: Craig, Danny, me, Dick, and Timmy.

I am opening the front door to my house.
Only the shell of the house remained standing.

I was so glad the boys could see for themselves the hardship the people had back then. The oldest son had the responsibility to stay and take care of the farm. That's why Pakie never came to America. The farmers had to wake up early in the morning and work all day, feeding the cows and other animals, bailing the hay, cutting the turf, letting it dry, then stacking it in piles, carrying the turf cart back to the house, and storing it for winter. There was also slaughtering the cows, and other animals so we had food to eat.

After we left the fields we went to the barn where one of the cows was having a baby. We were so excited and nervous because this was something the boys had never seen before. Well, it took a long time and nothing was happening. The word got out the cow was in trouble. Next, three or four more farmers came over to help. As soon as they got there, they took the cow, put her head in a brace and strapped the rest of her body tightly to the wall. Next, they got an object and helped pull the baby calf out. We were all holding each other tightly. The calf slammed onto the ground with a thud! We thought it was dead! Pakie told us if it was a female, they were going to name it Christine after me. However, it was a male so it was named Christopher! We all thought the baby wasn't going to make it. We went back to the house and said a little prayer for Christopher, but Pakie stayed in the barn most of the night. The next day, we walked up to the barn and there they were — Mother and son — doing beautifully, the baby drinking milk from its mother and jumping around. We were so relieved and happy!

That night we all went to Harrington's Pub, and my son Timmy played the bagpipes. He was great! Everyone loved it! Later they told us that Timmy was the first person to play the pipes in the pub.

Starting at the bottom: Craig, me, Dick, Danny, and Timmy behind Clooncunny School.

Passing of Pakie

A few years ago, we got word from Ireland that Pakie was very sick with cancer and in the hospital. Noel, Maggie, and I flew over. We stayed with Mary Frances and their son Johnny and his wife, Angela. We went to the hospital right away and as soon as he saw us, he was so happy. We stayed a week and went to see him as much as we could. On our last visit at the hospital, Noel, Maggie, and I gathered around Pakie's hospital bed and without any words being said, we knew this was the last time we would see him. Each one of us said our goodbyes because we knew we had to go back home to our families. When we left, he had a smile on his face, and I think he was at peace.

About six weeks later, we got a call from Mary Frances that he had passed away. Maggie and I flew back for the funeral. At the mass, I was asked to read a passage from the Bible and as I looked out over the church, it was packed with people. There were people there from all over the area. Some were all dressed up in their Sunday clothes, and then there were men in their wellingtons (boots) who had come in from the fields to honor him. He was so well loved and admired by the community and everyone knew what a great and honorable man he was. Since that last visit Johnnie and Angela have been blessed with a beautiful daughter. I'm sure Pakie would have been so proud.

I have not been back to the farm since then. It seems strange, but I feel telling my little story about my family has given me closure and peace. When I look back, I see us all together as one. Lily, the oldest, took over and raised us after my mother's death. Nellie, Terry, and Winnie helped her raise us also. Pakie and my father were always out working the farm (with Noel's help) from early morning until night. Maggie and I helped as much as we could by gathering the eggs, picking the berries from the trees, (especially gooseberries) and other little chores. And of course Uncle Jimmy was always telling us little stories and giving us little goodies if he could find some. Attracta was doing fine and liked where she was living.

Pakie and his dog Daisy.

Maggie and I are on our last trip to Ireland.
We were there for the passing of Pakie.

The Grandchildren

Years ago Dick and I were at a St. Patrick's Day Parade in West Orange. Our oldest son Danny came across the street to meet us and said he wanted to introduce us to someone. He took her hand and said, "This is Beth Boylan." I said, "Is your father John and your mother Mary who owned the Kandy Kane?" She said, "yes," and I couldn't believe it! She was the baby of the family. So many years had passed, and they were all grown up now. Danny and Beth started going out and soon started going steady. They then got engaged and married. Their daughter Maggie is my first grandchild.

Craig met Tara and had two beautiful children: Natalie and Ryan.

Timmy was the next to marry. He met Lisa and they have three beautiful children. Caitlyn, Tim, and Henry. Every day all the grandchildren give me so much joy!

Our family: I am with Lisa, Tara, Craig, Danny, Beth, Henry, Timmy, Maggie, Ryan, Tim, Catey, and Natalie, celebrating Easter Sunday.

From left: Beth, Tara, me, Danny, Craig, Timmy, Maggie, Lisa, Catey, Ryan, Tim, Natalie, and Henry. This is about a year ago, and we were in New York after just seeing the Christmas Show.

From left: Ryan, Maggie, Catey, Timmy, Natalie, Henry, celebrating Natalie's First Holy Communion.

My husband Dick passed away June 27, 2014 after a long illness. While he was in a care facility, there was a knock on the door. We all happened to be there that afternoon. We said, "Come in." And then we heard in an Irish brogue the priest who asked, "Is there a Mr. Mulvaney in this room?" Dick had been asleep, but all of a sudden he woke up and sat up on the bed and said, "Yes, Father, that's me." Well, the priest went over and kissed him on the forehead and then gave him Holy Communion. He said, "God bless you and now go back to sleep." They shook hands, and I knew Dick was at peace.

He was such a presence in everyone's life, especially his grandchildren. Anyone who met him loved him and knew they could depend on him. He was the best husband, father, and friend anyone could have, and he will never be forgotten.

After the service at the cemetery we all got back in our cars, and there was a knock on the window. It was the funeral director. We rolled the window down, and he said, "Chris, before you go I just wanted to let you know that when I called the Sergeant of Police for a police escort to the cemetery, he said sure and asked about how many cars there would be. When I told him about 178, well, the Seargent was in shock and said, "Is it a Dignitary, or is it the Pope?" He'd never had that many cars for the procession unless it was for someone really special. (I think we now know how much Dick was really loved.)

Then we all went back to the restaurant. After eating I heard a beautiful voice and I turned around and got up. Standing on the dance floor was my granddaughter Catey, who was 11 at the time, singing "Amazing Grace." It was so beautiful, and she did a great job.

When she finished everyone was clapping, and I started to walk back to my seat. All of a sudden I felt a tug at my dress, when I looked down I saw my grandson Henry who was 5 years old. He said, "Oh Grandma, I'm sooo sad," and he had tears in his little eyes. I said, "Why, what is the matter, Henry?" He said, "Well, now that Grandpa is gone, who is going to take care of you??" I had to think awhile because I didn't want to upset him so I knelt down and said, "You know my brother, Uncle Noel, right?" and he said "Yes" and then I said "Well he told me he would come to my house every day and take out the papers and the garbage and anything else that has to be done for me." Well... he looked at me and thought awhile and then gave me a big hug and said "Oh Grandma, I feel so much better now!!" and he put a big smile on his face and hugged me and then ran off and continued playing. My heart was bursting, and I got all choked up, there was so much love in his little face. How does a 5-year-old think of such things? It amazed me.

To this day, Noel still comes to my house and takes the newspapers out for me. One day he called and asked me if I needed anything done, and I told him no and that everything was OK. He replied, "Well, I don't want Henry to be mad at me if I don't do my chores." We both laughed.

Thankful and Loved

Now when I get together with my brother and sisters, we reminisce and laugh about all the fun we had in Ireland. We were so poor yet it never seemed to really matter! We had a wonderful mother and father that loved ALL of us and gave us all they could, with what little they had. All they ever wanted was to give us a better life!

I am so thankful that I came to my Cousin Betty's house. Everyone was welcomed there. One day many, many years later she was sitting on my bed while I was getting dressed for my son Danny's wedding — we were talking and she said, "Do you remember the first time you called me "Mommy"? And I said, "I don't think so," and she said, "It was the day when Ellen and you were making your first Holy Communion. We were standing in the living room by the stairs getting dressed. You said to me: 'Mommy, would you comb my hair, and I'll run upstairs to get my sweater?' Well, we both stopped for a minute and looked at each other, and then you realized what you had said, and we started laughing." That was the first time, and from that day on, she was Mommy to me. After she told me that story, she broke down in tears, and I went over to her, sat on the bed next to her, put my arms around her, gave her a kiss on the cheek, and said thank you for all you've done for me. I Love You. We both cried a little that day.

Without Mommy (Betty), Daddy (Freddy), Aunt Annie (Mama), Uncle Joe (Papa) I don't know what would have become of me and my family. I am so truly grateful for all that's been given to me. I had a wonderful husband of 52 years whom I loved, 3 beautiful sons and their wives, and 6 adorable, happy, and healthy grandchildren.

A Wonderful Life

Noel and I were raised with Ellen and Betty Ann. Mommy and Daddy treated us all the same. Growing up, if I ever got sad about something or wished that my mother and father were here with me — especially when my kids were growing up or I was experiencing something I had no control over — I would always think of my parents and know that they never abandoned me or purposely gave me away. They had no choice. It was not up to them but to God, and they did everything humanly possible to keep us all together. When I think of them, I know they were always there with me and never left me. They always loved me as well as my brothers and sisters. Over the years those thoughts have kept me going many times.

Remembering a Dream

One night, I remember having a vivid dream. I was sitting outside an ice cream shop at a little table and all of a sudden I saw Nellie and Winnie walking down the street toward me (They had both passed on by then), and I couldn't believe my eyes. They came over to me, and we were hugging, and I was so happy to see them! They looked like they both were in their twenties. Both of them were so beautiful, Nellie with her smile and Winnie with her long hair. I asked them where they were going, and they said they were taking the bus that was there. I said, "Oh, good!" I'll go with you, knowing if I did, we were going to have a wonderful time together.

I started to walk with them to the bus. They both held my hand and said, "No, you can't come with us this time, but don't worry. When you're ready, we'll be back to get you, and we'll never leave you again." I remember waving goodbye to the bus and them waving back, and I wasn't sad or afraid because I knew then what they were saying.

Someday, we all will be together again...

Pride of my Life

My name is inscribed on the Immigrant Wall of Honor at Ellis Island. I am so proud of that. I have participated in associations and activities that celebrate my Irish culture since childhood — attending numerous parades, fundraisers, benefits and dances. I am dedicated to my Irish Heritage and my community through my commitment to helping others. I have been an active member of the Women of Irish Heritage of the Jersey Shore since its inception. I also won the award for the "Women of the Year" in 2011. I also serve on the board for the non-profit "Just Us Girls" philanthropic organization assisting women and men struggling with breast cancer. This is our 21st Year.

About the Author

I was born in Ireland and came to this country when I was 9 years old. I lived with my aunt and uncle in West Orange, New Jersey. I went to Our Lady of Lourdes Grammar School until the 8th grade and then went to Edison Junior High for the 9th grade. I spent 10th, 11th, and 12th grade at West Orange High School. After high school I went to work for an insurance company doing typing. I stayed there until I got married and had my first child. Then I stayed home to raise my boys Danny, Timmy, and Craig. When Craig started school full time, I got part-time jobs with an agency, and then finally when the boys got older I took a full-time job. I worked for Atlantic Mutual Insurance Company. I started working as a secretary and then got promoted to Administrative Assistant to the Vice President of the Company. I stayed there until I moved to the shore with my family.